Reminisce with a Goddess

LaNane Woods

authorHOUSE®

AuthorHouse™
1663 Liberty Drive
Bloomington, IN 47403
www.authorhouse.com
Phone: 1-800-839-8640

Published by AuthorHouse 3/25/2011

ISBN: 978-1-4567-3700-9 (sc)
ISBN: 978-1-4567-3701-6 (e)

Library of Congress Control Number: 2011902348

Part
One
Just
~ 4 ~
Fun

Shuga

I went and spent a bella day with Nae

Awhile by her side I dedicated anyway

She is my Shuga Cane, bae-bae

7/17/10

<u>Beijo Louco</u>

Everyone thinks I've gone crazy

My mind's in Lynx crown me "Daisy"

Super high jinks I'm in Italy

La-Nane, Inc. soon in Valise

I'll even speak in Portuguese

Betcha weak when I say "beije-me"

8/15/10

<u>Fight</u>

It's our civil right

To wear black and white

While on a flight

To watch a night fight

Then later reunite

To have a pillow fight

Before we say goodnight

Alright

8/17/10

<u>Haters Ideas</u>

Here is a wave to all my haters

Don't be enslaved be a creator

Do not just rave be a translator

Don't misbehave be a debater

~ Or ~

Maybe you'll just stay a spectator

8/18/10

Part
Two
Déjà
Vu

<u>Trophy</u>

Many have been in search of me

They see a physique of a foxy lady

In "The Land of the Free"

They shout for "Victory"

But do they really

Want me

~ Or ~

A trophy?

7/10/10

<u>Heaven Sent</u>

Aviating through Bekaa

An angel fell to Ghana

In search to find his ghada

Bringing peace of mind across the Oceana

Please bear in mind the nirvanas

Be in her right mind an Americana

8/21/10

<u>Boo</u>

I exist by what I live up to

Could this be a far cry from déjà vu

In a blink of an eye I'll come through

Feels like Senior High I'm going to

I get tongue tied when I extend to you

I abide by your point of view

By and by I look up to you

Everything I need is in you boo

8/22/10

<u>Coexist</u>

Not to astray or be dismissed

I resist being last on your list

It's because I truly insist

Not to be betrayed but to coexist

And only to portray a heavenly bliss

8/30/10

<u>Security</u>

You're mighty and strong

I'm itsy and bitsy

When bleak with love you help me find security

You're a man and I a woman

Neither a trophy

You're love is the reason

Why my aura stays glistening

7/10/10

<u>Déjà Vu</u>

At full speed I'm good for you

I exude you I bleed blue

These trees surpass common mood

Emotions stampede are misconstrued

Please proceed and then carry through

Conquer, Secede its Déjà Vu

8/15/10

<u>Mz. Me 2</u>

Every time you desire me I want you

Every time you call me I come through

Every time you ask me I live up to

Every time you hold me I come to

Every time you kiss me I appeal too

Every time you adore me I cherish you

Every time you love me I love you too

8/14/10

<u>In Love</u>

In love with you I found my mind

Angle of view we've intertwined

Muscle into not to be left behind

Out of the blue? It's undefined!?

8/14/10

<u>Cherish</u>

Falling in love again

He only wants a friend

Seeing miracles had me feeling

Like he's created for healing

How do I resist?

I don't I cherish

8/9/10

<u>Thx</u>

Guaranteed blissfulness

Do you like a gal like this?

Handle what I've got to give

Forever you'll thank God to live

7/11/10

<u>Wishes</u>

I wish I could be "Kool"

I wish I wasn't "Old School"

I wish I wasn't "So Cute"

I wish I had the majority rule

I wish I could be wooed

I wish I had common good

I wish I understood

I wish I smelled incent wood

I wish I wasn't so hood

8/14/10

<u>Miracles</u>

I sincerely want to love you

But what you really want to do

Going to witness miracles in this world it's true

Always had you in my plans too

Prove how much you love your boo

7/10/10

10 Commandments

I love you – Enjoy me

I love you – Need me

I love you – Enlighten me

I love you – Consider me

I love you – Conquer me

I love you – Restore Me

I love you – Keep me

I love you – Spoil me

I love you – Kiss me

I love you – Love me

7/11/10

Me

Forgive me for being blue

Forgive me for needing you

Forgive me for missing your touch

Forgive me for thinking of you so much

Forgive me for being a tool

Forgive me for being cruel

Forgive me for my self-centered love

Forgive me for being emotional

Forgive me for being obstinate

Forgive me for my psychological state

Forgive me for when I cry for you

Do you forgive me yet, boo?

7/9/10

<u>True Love</u>

My freckled Goddess

No need to be anxious

At his best true love will manifest

7/9/10

Part
Three
`G

<u>Trillion</u>

You're heartening not a taboo

You're God's son sincere and true

Within a trillion you're my boo

I am no one without you

It's an uncommon breakthrough

Not a fiction of how-to

Nor even a to-make-do

It's a deepen love which we knew

And now a fortune collecting revenue

8/30/10

Happy Place

Here is a fella who spreads joy he's the real mccoy

More than twice I've been enticed to set foot in paradise

Despite the late nights he's a supreme delight

Plenty and mighty he guarantees tranquility

This Buddha has commas' in her nirvana

When people walk by and wonder why I smile

Without disgrace I look them in their face

And let them know of my happy place

12/14/10

N.A.T.

I'm a provider! Do you see?

I'll fill your purse with currency

I see your spirit is truly carefree

That's why I quickly

Made you my baby

Why wait for eventually?

When I want you for eternity

7/9/10

<u>Chant</u>

I love you! Love me.

I love you! Love me.

I love you! Love me.

I love you!

Do you love me, yet?

9/2/10

<u>Code 4</u>

WATCH!?.

When you close your eyes, you'll see

I'm "The Right One" a guarantee

Lady your first next turn is mine

You're my freckled Goddess tatted up and old' so fine

I'm here to see your dreams come true

You're my baby and I'm always your boo

7/8/10

<u>Integrity</u>

He's leading a brand new life

It's a big test!

He arrest those who've transgressed

Didn't want to hurt you

~ But ~

I was oppressed

Needing you badly

Do I dare suggest?

7/8/10

<u>Sweetness</u>

You're sweet to me

Believe in destiny

It be so cool "u & me"

We'd live together so happily

7/12/10

<u>Divinity</u>

The gate to the Great Divine

I found through your eyes

In the sky our souls intertwine

In our hearts and minds

We don't take time to remind

That it's us in this geodesic line

8/8/10

I Luv U

When I smile

You're the reason why

"Forever u & me"

We're supposed to be

I love you in everyway

Nothing left to say

7/11/10

(ˇvˇ)
( )
(..)(..) ♥

<u>Destiny</u>

How can I verbalize?

These feelings are

Hard to describe!

Sweet destiny

I knew love would

Find me eventually

No need for the toxicology

What we feel is naturally

In our body

6/15/10

<u>Promises</u>

Spend your life with me

Exclusively "u & me"

With all reciprocity

I'll promise security

7/12/10

<u>Happy</u>

Big Daddy on the scene

Waiting to see who's ready

Won't keep any who appear

Bossy, needy, cheeky or pushy

Big Daddy says it's easy

To be happy

7/17/10

Hi-Po

I saw you in my dreams last night

I risked my life to be by your side

How amazing it was to see it playing in my mind

I could see you clearly reaching from aside

Offside or roadside you're worth any risk as defied

7/8/10

<u>Roger That</u>

You're beyond my goal

You'll have me speaking in Espanol

You own my body and soul

We'll need crowd control

When you enter your rabbit hole

8/8/10

`G

He's like a `G

His love's in me

He believes in destiny

~ A.B.C. ~

It's elementary

It be like eating from the chocolate tree

And or sipping coffee or tea

He's so damn sweet to me

8/14/10

<u>High</u>

I'm tryn to keep you mine

As long as we are spending time

You are always on my mind

Your love gets me so high

But so what your love is mine

9/14/10

<u>Us</u>

Your whole life you've been mine

We sacrifice time to be side by side

Don't deny that our souls entwine

No need to seek and find

Love is our blessing from the divine

7/11/10

Part
Four
Adored

<u>Wise Guy</u>

Excuse me for not getting along

Excuse me for crying to every song

Excuse me for the long sigh

Excuse me Mr. Wise Guy

Excuse me! "...it was lust..."!?!

Excuse me but where's the trust?

Excuse me for pushing you away.

Excuse me but you're not worthy anyway.

Excuse me! "I never meant much..."?

Excuse me but get in touch.

Excuse me! "...it was just sex..."!?!

Excuse me for being so damn vexed.

Excuse me if we never meet again.

Excuse me but we aren't even friends.

Excuse me for my exotic looks.

Excuse me while I look through my little black book.

8/31/10

<u>Your Way</u>

I may only be in your way

To what degree will I portray?

I will only be in your way

An old story with all cliché

I would only be in your way

I'll disagree on a good day

I must have only been in your way

A devotee without delay

I shall only be in your way

An appointee with hell to pay

I ought to be in your way

I'm not a trophy that goes astray

I opt to be in your way

I'm an absentee a blink away

8/29/10

<u>Who You</u>

Don't know me?

I'm your baby!

Don't know you?

You be my, boo!

Don't know!?

But anyway...

Who has time to play?

7/17/10

<u>A Friend</u>

Been a decade never thought I'd love again

Alhamdulillah!! He has forgiven our sins

The goose bumps we feel are epiphanies

Not "The Honeymoon Syndrome" fantasies

They say "All good things come to an end"

Wishing we could have been just a friend

7/4/10

Q's: & A:

What is your interpretation?

Could it be infatuation?

Maybe it's a bazaar exposition?

Or even a fool's proclamation?

Patience is a process of love's manifestation.

7/11/10

<u>Dreaming</u>

You're everything I've fanaticized

At first I didn't recognize

When I opened my eyes

It was you to my surprise

No lie you're my type of guy

Still dreaming?

Am I!?

7/11/10

<u>Childish</u>

Today I feel melancholy

My boo says I intervene

No more time we're spending

Well maybe

If I show more maturity

7/17/10

Gabby

Dingy, Gabby or Clingy!

Omit what your love does to me

Are you ready to see?

Look deeply inside this little lady

But your remedy was to set me free

You will always be

The one for me

~ Gaby ~

7/8/10

<u>Beautiful Lies</u>

Do I apprehend my boyfriend?

And pretend there's a big diamond ring?

To prove my love and affection

~ Or ~

Is this the bitter- sweet

End of rejection?

8/15/10

U.T.L.

You said you'll never leave

Now you're turning your back on me

Stay with me and accept my apology

Don't leave!

It's the anxiety in me

Please say you'll always stay

Don't let our love slip away

7/9/10

<u>Missing Person</u>

Dreading of being on my own

I'm afraid of being alone

When I cry at night

I hold my pillow tight

You're too good to be true

Don't let me wake up from you

7/8/10

<u>Bye</u>

Silly to think that I

Could keep you for my guy

I must have been blind

Lucent and just out of my mind

Before you finish this rhyme

We've already said our goodbyes

7/11/10

C' Ya

Respect my space.

Don't suffocate me!

I'll find a man when I'm ready

Besides you probably

Say that shyt to everybody

I think you're sexy and intelligent Yes! Far from being dumb

Ultimately you're emotionally drained and romantically numb

Catch your bus sir every 15 minutes one is sure to come

7/8/10

<u>Loved</u>

He loved me once

I love him in abundance

With so much brilliance

Wish he'd learn patience

No time to be his guidance

Don't want to be in avoidance

But I'll stay in silence

He must learn perseverance

7/11/10

<u>You</u>

I'm the hymn without your voice

I'm the vote without a choice

I'm the tiger without a growl

I'm the lining without a cloud

I'm the Goddess without a heaven

I'm the eight without the seven

I'm the dog without a bone

I'm the earth without the ozone

I'm the yin without you yang

I'm the gun without the bang

I'm the vanity without the vain

I'm the medallion without a chain

I'm the wish without the star

I'm the string without a guitar

I'm the purple without the blue

I'm the one who needs you

8/8/10

<u>S.O.S.</u>

Saving your mind

I'd go crazy sometime

Can't you recognize?

Then open your eyes

I pray we'll survive

7/11/10

```
        UUUUUUUUU
     UUUUUUUUUUUUUUU
   UUUUUUU2222222UUUU
  UUUUUU222I22222UUUUU
 UUUUUU22222222222UUUUUUUUU
UUUUU2222222222222UU222222222UUU
UUUUU22222222LUV2222222222222222UU
UUUUU22222222222222222222222222   UUU
 UUUUU222222222222222U22222222   UUU
  UUUU22222222222222222222222     UUU
  UUUU2222222222222222222222      UUU
   UUUU22222222222222222         UUU
    UUU222222222222222         UUUU
     UUUU2222222222         UUUU
      UUUUUU2222          UUUUU
       UUUUUU          UUUUUUU
        UUUUUUUUUUUUUUU
        UUUUUUUUU
        UUUUUU
        UUUU
        UU
        U
         I
          I  I
           I
            I I
             I I
              I
               I
              I
             I
            I
           I
          I
           I I
               I
```